I AIN'T LUKE WARM!

A Collection of Poetry

BY

KATHY A. BROCKS

AF471879

I AIN'T LUKE WARM!

A Collection of Poetry
BY
KATHY A. BROCKS

ISBN : 978-0-557-56800-0

Revised 2010
Kathy Brocks, Author
kathyabrocks@gmail.com
P.O. Box 353
Elgin, IL 60121

Special Preface
Words to you!

Some of the poems in this book were written prior to my getting saved and the others after I got saved. I admit I loved going to the clubs staying out all night hanging out with friends. Truly I just wanted to dance and really did not care about anything else. Dancing was the only freeing thing you could not get arrested for doing.
After I got saved I still loved dancing I just changed how I dance but the ferver was still intense. I just switched it up to formulated styles like, Salsa, Meringue, Reggae, Bachata, Stepping, a little Jazz and Freestyle minus sexual overtones, hallelujah dancing only. Generally, I just let the Holy Ghost take over. Not everyone rolls on the floor when the Holy Ghost inspires dances of praise.

I write to express myself because sometimes it's easier to write it down rather than say it aloud or it brings a faster release. You don't have to argue or fornicate for some, so no need to repent for a brief moment of anger.
Just saying the name, Jesus, bring instant relief.
But you also want to learn how to make good decisions like Jesus.
To make it cool consider yourself a rapper, word-smith, a human thesaurus that earns dollars. Whatever you do work on keeping it clean. Build your vocabulary so you don't have to swear to get your point across.

Rules of the (Christian) Road

At first it seems rather hard to stay in the mainstream of Christianity. To be more than just a good Christian is the goal of the majority of Christians. It's a what can I do or how can I help attitude. However the goal is to stay on this road but act in the same place as yesterday. So, what can we as Christians do to move ahead in our walk? There are several things. But before we do anything we've got to go to God and prostrate ourselves, you know, pray.

Third, you say, "Lord I come into your presence through the shed blood of your son, Jesus Christ". And since 90% of prayer is petition bring fourth your petitions.

Ask God for everything that is in your heart and if you just don't know what to ask for call on the Holy Spirit of God to intercede in your behalf. And even if you know what you want to do to be a blessing to the church but don't know how to go about it, pray. Ask God for guidance and then begin to act on that prayer. You can go to your Cell Leader or Pastor and tell them of your desire and they will assist you. Sometimes the areas in which we desire to work have yet to be established or are in the making. If it's in the process then ask if you can assist with the process. However, if it doesn't exist then create it, with the permission of the Pastor.

WAIT! You say Start it, ask for help. I just got saved. I don't even know what I'm doing. All I know is that I get up and comb my hair every morning and hope I don't end up dead on some street corner. I answered the alter call because what the preacher was saying seemed better than how I was living. I just got tired of being afraid. Now, all I have is just another fear. It's different but it's still a fear. I fear failing at this new job as a

Christian. It's is a job right just like anything else I have to work at it. I don't feel equipped.

These concerns are so real. Everybody feels this way whether they are new to Christ, a backslider and sometimes those that have walked with Christ for all of their lives. However the latter is not to scare you but is sometimes just a fact. It's partly being attacked by Satan and just not being equipped from the beginning.

When a person first gives themselves to God it's like walking through a smoke filled room and exhaling at the clearing or just knowing it's okay to jump off of the teeter totter. You stand alone at the alter but you feel as though you've just married an entire clan.

You're all excited you don't know what to do first, should you tell your best friend, tell your mom. You've got to tell someone you feel like you're going to burst. So, you run outside and scream to the world, "I'm free!!!!!!!! I'm free!!!!! Thank you Jesus. I'm free""""

Now as the police at concerts say, "It's time for crowd control". You need to be taught to scream your salvation in more than just belching it out to the world. The after taste should last longer than a two minute song. This is where the soul warriors come into play. "Soul Warriors" are Christ's soldiers, children of God, winners of souls for Christ, your brothers and sisters in Christ, what they do is win souls for Christ first and then maintain and build up or edify you so that you may be know the truth and trust in God always and for all things just as Jesus did. The goal is to be like Jesus, to be a citizen of the kingdom of God and to get you where Jesus is now. The veterans or soul warriors minister to you just as the Lord did to Jesus and Jesus to his disciples and they did to each other. You are taken in under the wings of a brother or sister in Christ and he, she or they will teach you how to live a Christian life. No, you won't be in a commune. Where you live is your decision. But, you will have to make some changes in your daily life. No, you shouldn't be asked to give away all of your money. God only required 10% of your gross income, which is called tithing. Tithes are used to maintain the church. The Pastor's salary comes from this, the utilities, advertising, blessings to help those less fortunate.

The brethren will answer any questions you may have regarding the word of God, the Bible. Yes, you will be asked to read your bible. Not everyone starts out reading the bible daily but it helps. Reading the word of God is a vital tool used in prayer. Knowing the word of God strengthens your knowledge of God, and increases your prayer ability. Simply put, you have more to pray about. In the word it illustrates how God not only desires fervent prayer but God also requires variety. And variety comes through the knowledge of God and knowledge through reading the word of God.

Prayer

Romans 8:26

In the same way, the spirit helps us in our weakness. We do not know what we ought to pray for, but the spirit himself intercedes for us with groans that words cannot express

Five finger prayer method spend five minutes on each finger this should get you to 25-30 minutes. Each day increase each finger by five minutes. There is no real limit this is to get you to pray for at least an hour.

1st – Thumb Since this is the closest to you it is for friends, family, neighbours.

2nd – Index Pray for those that guide or teach you. Your mentors, Pastor, Church leaders etc.

3rd - Middle Finger Is for governmental leaders, people in authority

4th - Fourth or Ring Finger those who are sick, homeless etc.

5th- Pinky FingerPray for Yourself

Prayer is speaking to God. You are speaking to a higher being, higher than man. When we pray we are showing our need for God. You get restoration wisdom, healing, overcome the devil and meets needs through prayer.

First acknowledge God by meditating on God. Second, anticipate God being with you. Third, come with desire .have a deep longing to speak with God. Fourth, pray with fervency.

Auspicious

Let me tell you how awesome my God is
He picked me up from despair
He brushed me off
He held me close
Then he showed me just how much he loved me
Then he gave me the challenge of seeking him always
He blessed me with kindness and mercy
He gave me joy in times of turbulence
He made me steady
He gave me peace
He made me whole

Christ's Crow's Feet

Before his ascension
Jesus Christ had crows feet
Bowel movements
Greasy hair
Dirty teeth
Soiled feet
Pimples and hair bumps
Unwashed hands, dirty nails
Like you and me
Except
He's a diety, a Son of the most high
Not by happenstance
But by free will
He came
And opened himself up
So that we may be blessed
With all his might he absolved us
With all his might he linked us to our
Home once again

Blind Faith

**You are an embryonic suckling
Being stretched and molded
Into a helpless, needy, trusting
Wonder
You need help to eat
Stay clean and safe
You don't even breathe on your own
Some days you can barely open your eyes**

**Your first six years are filled with play, laughter, innocence
And unrelenting curiosity of everything around you seen and unseen
You have this ability to discern right from wrong**

**The next six years you develop bonds
You learn new things**

**The next six you're all grown up
Confused
What is this?
What am I suppose to be
What am I suppose to do**

**You go to your friends, Teachers, Social clubs, etc.
Except your everlasting counsellor**

**I've sat beside you since before you were conceived
I've sat beside you even when you didn't believe
I've walked with you down dark alleys
Stood next to you when thought you heard something
Under your bed
I've never left you**

**Deliverance will come when you seek me
Deliverance will come when you open your heart to me
Deliverance will come with humility
Deliverance will come when you bow down and give praise unto me
Deliverance will come by your faith**

Color

The colors of my heart are:

J.E.S.U.S.

J…he justifies my faith, fills me from within

E…everlasting is he that descended for you and me

S…sanctuary of hope, love, mercy and grace….wide are his arms stretched across the heavens reaching into the unheavenly places…

U…unyielding roots in my soul not grappling for control

S….healing spiritual intercession with destination at hand soaring up and under this great vast creation you are leading the master plan

Dinner Time

My days are amid
A bubble, a fragile
Particle of water blended
With a variety of chemical
I want to set adrift
On a boat with no particular
Destination
Wake to the beautiful blue hovering over and angelic clouds
Parting for the morning Sun
I would live like a scavenger
upon the sea
I would hunt like
The searchers of Moby Dick
With spears sharpened to
Split a hair
My pasture of perfection,
Hip forward like a gun fighting
Ballerina, waist twisted
With the wind
Spear is in the left hand
Prey is in sight
He circles the boat with great emotion…
You pull back as if a bedspring or automatic
Door
He circles once more keeping his eye on the deadly
Spear
Just as he rounds the side
You are his blind spot
You release with minute speed
The spear soars
Through
The thick ocean air
A slim line of blood stretching an inch long races
Upward on the wood of the spear
Dinner time
There's nothing
Like freshly fried silver bass

EL' AQUI SIEMPRE

If I were on the tip top of a mountain peak
Staring down and had to chose whether
To turn left or right I would pray
First because even the most simple
decisions can have a profound
affect on your life. Its choosing to remain in a quandary
or press forward to the unknown trusting in the Lord all the way

It's believing he is there for me even though
He is no longer flesh, tangible
Its feeling his strong arms wrapped around
me holding me tight and not letting go, comforting me
allowing me to let go and just do an absolute free fall
and being caught by more than a strand of my hair
but by the palm of his mighty hands
he's like a great big teddy bear you snuggle up next to
wants others to see how much you love with enormous joy

It's knowing he's with you when you strut down the street.
In your favorite suit
Or when you are down in the dirt digging
Holes for your plants or mending a fence
He is always here… there…I love him so…

ELOHIM

He stamps with Lamentations
Of his love
Agaupe in every sense
Opening your innocence
Follow me he commands
Be as a child
Open to receive
Accepting me freely
Doubting not 'til
Impious crows tug
Increasing your temptations
Leading you away from your salvation
Rising like a luminescent edifice
Birthing your limbs to stone
Feeding you a mirage
Of weed turned green
Fruitless in kind
Never building on the inheritance
Of yours and mine
Fleeting at the sound of the horn
Torting the "Word" he plays with you
Being created he can't hold you
You belong to the God of many names
One and the same, Elohim.

Everyday weaves new beginnings

Oh love usher me into the sweet
Aroma of his presence
Lips beaming
Brow dripping
Your faithfulness consuming
Your words rising up in me
Like a twinkling morning star
You remain with your eyes in my full sight
How lovely they are speckled with colors
Of the rainbow watching over me
Communicating with me
Inquiring of my desires as I scratch
The stubble on my face
Oh how I ache to hold you near
When I know you need me to stay away
It is with love we usher each other
Into God's loving arms
It is because of his love I am able to keep you in my heart
It is because of his love you still accept all of me
I love you dearly
You are the light in my skies
Thank you for choosing me

Genesis 2:7

You gave me life
You gave me a reason to believe
You gave me life
You gave me your son
He prostrated himself from you to me
So I'd have a reason to believe
You gave me life
You breathed life into me

I AM

I AM OMNIPOTENT

I AM THE PRESENT IN THE EVERLASTING

I AM THE "A" IN WAS

I AM YOUR PROVIDER

I AM YOUR COUNSELOR

I AM YOUR THERAPIST

I AM YOUR DOCTOR

I AM ALL THE RICHES YOU SEEK

I AM THE CATACISMIC EXPLOSION THAT ROCKS

YOUR MIND

I AM THE EUPHEMISTIC INTERLUDE THAT PULLS YOU NEAR

WITH EVERY WORD AND EVERY BREATH YOU TAKE

WITH EVERY THOUGHT YOU THINK

I DWELL IN THE INNATENESS OF YOUR SOUL

I HEAL THE SATANIC PEARLS ERODING YOUR FLESH

I EXEMPLIFY ALL THAT TAKE YOU OUT OF THE JUNGLES OF

UNCERTAINTY

ALL THAT KEEPS YOUR PALMS FACING UP

AND YOUR FEET PLANTED ON THE RIGHTEOUS PATH

I TOO TRAVELED LEAVING BEHIND THE SPIRIT

THAT LIVES IN ALL

"I am " Continued

IF ONLY YOU'D CALL

PRETEND I AM A FRIEND YOU HAVEN'T HEARD FROM IN A WHILE

PRETEND THE PHONE COMPANY HAS CALLED TO OFFER YOU A BETTER

WAY TO STAY IN CONTACT WITH THE ONE THAT

LOVES YOU IN SPITE OF ALL YOUR INIQUITIES

SEEKING ME IS YOUR BEST BET BECAUSE AFTER ALL

IS SAID AND DONE

I LOVE YOU MOST

WHO AM I

I GO BY MANY NAMES

WONDERFUL, COUNSELOR, THE EVERLASTING,

FATHER, THE PRINCE OF PEACE, INTERCESSOR, CONFORTER,

STAND-BY, COUNSELOR, STRENGTHNER, THE MIGHTY GOD

I AM NO WONDER

I AM TRUE

I AM THE TRINITY

I AM YOUR CREATOR

I AM YOUR SAVIOR

I AM YOUR PROTECTOR

I AM THE WORD

I AM THE SON

I AM THE HOLY SPIRIT

"I am " Continued

I AM GOD

AND I SAY TO YOU

COME PRAY IN MY HOUSE

WORSHIP ME

FOR I AM ALL YOU SEEK

I WILL BIND ALL EVIL SPIRITS IF ONLY YOU'D SPEAK

TO ME

I AM THE LAW FOR IT IS WRITTEN

I DIED FOR YOUR SINS

SO NO MATTER WHAT YOU'VE DONE

YOU CAN ALWAYS COME HOME

BUT DON'T TAKE MY LOVE FOR STUPIDITY

FOR IF YOU FORSAKE I WILL COME DOWN ON YOU

LIKE A WRATH OF FIRE

LIKE A THIEF IN THE NIGHT

BY THIS YOU WILL DESTROY ALL YOUR BLESSINGS

I AM JOY

I AM LOVE

I AM THE SAME YESTERDAY, TODAY, AND EVERMORE

<u>I AM THE BREAD OF LIFE</u>

I am!
Continuous
I am!
Flowing

I am
Molding

I am
Merciful

I am
Gracious

I am the bread of (your) life
Kneading (your soul) over and over again
Created by God
Set inside of you
My holy spirit
Takes root
Cleansing
With every bend
As I stretch you
Into a humble mold
Of me, Jesus Christ
Your risen savior
Sustaining
With my water
I grow from within
Stretching from your heart
To the tips of your fingers
Down to the soles of your feet
Satisfying your
Every need
Providing your
Every desire
Tireless
I am!

Melted Butter

Sometimes it's salty
Sometimes it's hot
Other times it's sticky like
Melted movie popcorn butter
One after another
Flowing over the hills
And peaks
'Til the last
Accompanied by a whisper
A shadow of what was
Still falling over the mountains
And through the valleys
The best has already seen it's last

I Had A Dream

I had a dream that one day
I would stand before the crowd
And praise the Lord out loud (3x)

Growing in the glory of his love
Of it there's no wonder of
The power he holds in his hand
The creator of man
His words washes us clean
From commonality

I had a dream that one day
I would stand before the crowd
And praise the Lord out Loud (3x)

Filling his sons with his power of his blood
Preparing for the hour
Swooping up the few of his faithful children
He draws them up and spreads 'em across the heavens
Filing every prepared inch
Setting his children onto righteousness
That's the glory of his magnificence

NIGHT SCENE

Craving the night scene is like digging your own grave
You might as well stand in a ditch
As the earth rolls down your shoulders
The nights I spent hanging out were just a waste
I can no longer feel the vibe in my stomach
Or the smoke choking my face
God has brought me into a new place, a new place
The desire to seek him is all I crave

Craving the night scene is just a waste
Before he showed me grace
The quick grind of a rapid beat turned the stringy legs of the
Dancers, belly rolls of amateurs

Sticky syrupy jalapeno hot
More spice than I could handle

I craved it with all my being
Salt filled sweat dripping through my breast

S pongy shirt sticking to my back
Panties wet
Oh but I craved it

The noise, the noise engulfed me
I, He, We had to be there every weekend
Sometimes Wednesdays too

Smoke filled rooms filling my lungs burning my eyes
I had to have it, I craved it
The throbbing beat
The scratching twang
The quick beat of gyrating bodies
Swinging from the cages
Diving face first into the crowds
I craved it

Jealousies, rapid hearts beat
I craved it
Men fighting over me
I craved it

"Night Scene" Continued

Women looking intensely
I had to have it

I loved orange juice in mine
This made me want it just a bit more
Tipping, tipping, tipping over too far

The DJ's balcony I feared it
Because I craved it
No good for me but I craved it

All night long I stored it up
Hugging, pouncing, swinging and laying it
Oh baby, I craved it

My fingers hot sticky and wet
As I held his head where he laid it
This I, He, we made it because I craved it

I had to have this piece, this piece we shared
Because I craved the warm, steady pounding
Of his sweet, salty, sweaty—I craved it

Though I knew this direction wouldn't last long
I made the most of it. He wasn't going the direction I was going so I begged.

Love me the way you use too
I have no money but I love you

"Night Scene" Continued

I loved you but I, we couldn't stay together
Because I loved God more than you but I didn't know it
He was interceding as my grandfather prayed he'd do;
As our father said he'd do

Starving soon became my game plan
It was like a vampire needing blood

I needed the night air, the music, the frolicking untouched patty cake of it all
In one swoop I gave it up or so I thought.

One last event of frolic I succumbed to do
Smoke filled flashing lights swirling chasing the room
Pumped up thick in speech
Oh so sweet lips full of luscious nothings
I didn't crave it I tired to save it.
Him I wanted to keep but he wasn't for me
A perfection thanking God he wasn't dying I wanted him to fit

I was beginning to want it all over again but I got tired of dragging my foot around
Sometimes I'd see him in my sleep telling me the prize was within reach

You know that thing all belles desire from birth
So I gave it up
Confused at first for love I needed for love I did
But as time gained God became the trophy I gained
Nothing else I wanted so much than to know the prediction of his glory
Oh, I craved it
I needed to know what was this glory
They all spoke of with passion never seen
What was this glory as he pointed to me

I became a fetus pulling on the tube
Give me, give me what I need

I am craving you
Please I want to know this glory we seek
The smoke cleared the room
The light began to shine and
Soon I began to feel his perfect love
Unmatched by any man
I had to praise him, call on my inheritance
Yes, now I am craving him, my Lord and Savior, Jesus

PICTURE PERFECT

At last I found that special someone
At last I see why I waited
At first I thought it was all just talk
Now, I see, I see it wasn't just caddy women
Blowing smoke
At last, at last I can take air in and
Blow it out again and instead of it hitting the floor
It's balancing softly on his whiskered cheek
Mocha chocolate, black curly, finely groomed, shiny tart and ripe
With every breath the strength of his curl draws me nearer
All sounds one, all limbs intertwined
Stretching towards the head, sovereign of mine

Predictable

I once knew this girl
Hers was as short as rice
Her walk robust
Her body scared from head to toe

She wore bifocals
As thick as the soles of
Preppies shoes
Her hands wrinkle and slender
Her teeth all aglow of yellowing tartar
The black man's freckle
She wore studiously
And on corn ridden feet accompanied by a bunion or two she danced
The fools dance of her forgotten youth

Played she did gaily with the children of her siblings 'til nightfall
And off to bed for them all
Snugly she tucked them in after being washed and splattered with petroleum jelly
Exhausted from her labor of play
She laid down in dusty rags
Each night she went to sleep
She dreamed the same dream
Her playing with the children
Rushing them off to bed and
Wondering when their parents
Will come to get them
If at all

Sayings and Seeings!

Wrapped in cellophane
He sees the bridge behind you
Tall slender and erect it stands
Like soldiers on the front line
Decaying, crumbling, pressing on
Steadfast with one clear end in sight
Puddles of rational souls camouflaged with
A touch of pepper for seasoning
Galloping with the speed of a rocking horse
It rounds the turn
Continually ending in the same spot
Chaos, serenity and the guilt of experience
Wrapped in cellophane
Lead me out

When it gets Misty

Clouds are a mist
Of gas above the clutter
And the storm before the calm

The light of the nuances
The primer
The dichotomy
Of light and dark
The erosion of metals
And birth of new life

Clouds soothes the savages
And eludes the calm

Sugar

Men are like candy
They rot your teeth
Picking at your baseline
Roaming through the orifices
Connecting your mind
Binding a hold stronger
Than the twine of an unborn babe
Searching, fishing like a worm on a hook
Spreading jam everywhere they look

Men are like candy
They rot your teeth
Prancing to and fro
Never sure which way to go
Deception in the mind
Protected all the time
Always knowing what they want
Yet the game of taunting is a sport

The cloak and dagger of it all
Hides and binds the will of
the true seekers of the divine

The word fills all that they rot
Soothing and cooling the smoldering
Fire within giving the prey a place to land

Knowing that sugar rots the mind
All knowing ever true
He loves you through and through
He heals all that hurts
Never letting you feels the full
Strength of the wound
Filling you from within
Clinging and carrying
Through the wind
Never leaving
He loves you all the way
Because man is like sugar
On your teeth, they rot the mind

The "Word" frees you from the crowd

The "Word" frees you from the crowds
Of the inveterate* strains
The everyday things
Looping all you touch

The "Word" frees you from the crowds
Leading you down the path of righteousness
Comforting with a fiery storm of heart filled faith

The "word" frees you from the crowds
Knowing your every move all you do
Where you go giving you the choice

Flowing through heart
Swirling in your ear
The "Word" frees you from the crowds

Lifting you up from temptation
Leaving behind your old man
Never separating
The "Word" frees you from the crowds
Having all dominion
Honoring for believing
Punishing for envying

Thrusting into an unformed mass
Never attempt to deceive the kingdom is his
Life breathed to make you his

The "Word" frees you from the crowds
Next to perfection
He created once more
Giving you a reason for salvation
Loving you evermore
The "Word" frees you from the crowds

***Inveterate-persistent habits*

<u>White Harvest</u>
(John 4)

**It's like the blood of your menstrual on birth control,
Regulating
What more can I say than I have 'im
Just where I need him
Pumping through my veins
Relieving the strain
Every drip having a purpose
And every purpose a goal
Finely and tightly wound into a single thread
Soaring through your tunnels
Weaving in and out
Piercing my soul so that I
May be clean**

<u>Inspiration, let me be yours</u>

**The timbers and leave fall
Softly around it's roots
The wind gently carries them
Through the forest and along
The river banks dancing
Along the calm waters
Bright green stretched out strong
Slight moldings it travels
Down stream through rumbling
Waters popping, tossing, pushing
It along and over the falls a fifty foot
Drop to more thunderous waves
And rustling wind sliding it up on the
Soft dry grass next to a unique green one**

Upstage

In the theater upstage is the back and downstage is the front when facing the audience. Like an inverted pyramid. Note: this is an interpretation of various stories of the bible and personal accounts blended together.

I don't want to stand on a pulpit
I don't want to stand on a stage
Talking at the masses
I want to be among the crowd
Spreading the gospel of God

I want to feed the masses
Turkey and bologna sandwiches
With orange or grape pop with
A side of chips in a zip lock bag

I want to seek out the sick
And tap the strength within them
Straightening stuttering tongues
So that the words spoken become
As clear as silk when in his presence

Closing the flood gates of impure thoughts
Opening the gate for his love to flow freely
Into this readied heart

I want to be just like the only man ever
Born sin free

I ache and my lips begin to tremble my eyes
See an ugly deep dark frosty blue
If for a second my thoughts fall from his grace

Where is my kindness, where is my forgiving
And compassionate heart
Why have I stopped taking interest in others
Am I not refined,

Am I not a measure of effortless beauty of manner, form and style
To have some sense of propriety
Or has righteousness left me all together
Where, where, where are my standards he rooted in me

When I stray he pulls me back
Humbly " *i* " fall at his feet
Arms clenched around his legs
Tears and slobber of remorse cake his garment

Opening his heart for the seventieth time
He stretches out his hand with moans and groans
Which I do not understand to straighten out my twisted road

Smacking his hand I wobble along in my peripheral vision
Every other crate and every bottle top
A stumbling block locked in on all sides
With the top of my cage closing in
My stupor lifts
For half a second for my mouth to utter
Your powerful name
Jesus!

At last, the crackling of my outstretched arms brings a sigh of relief Lord
I am nothing without you
Pour into me your love
O righteous one
That I may bath in your splendor
Drink from your fountain

Let your word dissolve on my tongue
Like smooth grains of sugar
Sink into my flesh
Like melted Vaseline
I am your readied servant eyes seeing your face
Ears hearing your voice
Mouth speaking your word
Yesterday forgotten
Tomorrow is yours
Today I am standing in your field
Gathered with your faithful servants
Lord use me

Races

I'd walk a thousand miles to find a rolling brush
and only two for a movie

I'd dance until dawn
I'd go until dusk without a crust of bread
But only until 8pm without a life less touched

I'd run a thousand miles to get to the other side
Is it bait and switch or switch and bate

It's been so long
The color blurs in the light

How far will you go
Over the cliff or just to the neighborhood store

I travel not to my front door
If my perfume was less green
But around the world to catch a falling peddle

How far should I go to find a man so near
His breath mellow
Sweet like honey
I longed for him daily
Who know all I had to say
Is, "Jesus save me"
This trip would have ended
40 years ago
Why was I in such a hurry

Testimony

Awanjanne
Hola
Borjorno
Hey
Que tal

Yo levanter a saber
Dios es mucho grand
Dios es amore
Dios en mi
Dios en tu

Asi, yo saber
Que es testimonial para amore

God created me and you for a reason even if it's just to be a go between, a mediator
In this life I have learned that life is all too beautiful to concentrate on the negative
but too short to ignore the pain inflicted on others

What constitutes an ensemble is order
Organization is the thing that will push you further in all venture
If you fail to plan then you plan to fail
You can start with a simple thought, word, then just let everyone know your plan, your objective,
and there you have your plan has already been set in motion
stability attains the height of skies
lest there's a flaw
then it crumbles like a rock
under the fist of God
His love is strong but his might is destructive for the lazy
And contemptible of heart as well as the ornamental children of God

Sweet Surrender

Burning Hot summer mornings' sweet suckable dew rolling up
Your outstretched arms flailing in the musty sand strung wind
Cherry bomb cheeks swallow
A joyous hello
Feet stolen from a cartoon beat the tearless ground to flick
On the light bulbs of youths crunched down in alley ways, lounging in pool halls, arcades, strip clubs,
One by one his words rolled out of his mouth with a predetermined purpose, each word with a name attached to gather, cleanse and set free
From the massive weight
Wearing grooves in your shoulders
Where your muscles use to be
From the salted tongue vultures licking your wounds of old
From the hidden spikes ready to tear you a new hole
Sweet like the endless drippings of honey from a finely aged beehive
Gripping like the ground you kissed
'cause of the unexpected drive-bys
Sensuous like the way you really want but better
Comforting just the way you need
The hot has lost its stick
But the dew of his love remains

Other books by Author

"Reunite me with your breath once again: 12 Breath of God"

An intimate look into the lives of 12 ordinary people; one no better than the other; all looking for an escape, "Reunite Me with My Breath Once Again: 12 Breath of God" a quick journey to building trust and faith; realization that we are no greater than what we believe.

www.ingramcontent.com/pod-product-compliance
Ingram Content Group UK Ltd.
Pitfield, Milton Keynes, MK11 3LW, UK
UKHW041835200726
13854UKWH00003BA/1148